# Who Is That?

THE
LATE LATE
VIEWERS
GUIDE
TO THE OLD OLD MOVIE PLAYERS

By
**Warren B. Meyers**

Illustrated By
**Jerry Lang & Gösta Viertel**

GREENWICH HOUSE
Distributed by Crown Publishers, Inc.
New York

# ACKNOWLEDGEMENTS

Grateful thanks is hereby tendered to Cinemabilia,

The Memory Shop, The Movie Star News, and The Library of the Performing Arts at Lincoln Center,

for their cooperation in the securing of photographs.

The author also wishes to thank Bob Levin

for his unfailing technical wizardry, and imperturbable good humor.

Unfortunately, no amount of acknowledgement can ever

adequately repay the author's debt of gratitude to his wife,

Lorraine F. Meyers,

for her unstinting and invaluable assistance in the preparation of this book.

Copyright © MCMLXVI by Production Design Associates, Inc.
All rights reserved.
This 1982 edition is published by Greenwich House,
a division of Arlington House, Inc.,
distributed by Crown Publishers, Inc.,
by arrangement with The Citadel Press.
Manufactured in the United States of America

Library of Congress Cataloging in Publication Data

Meyers, Warren B.
Who is that?

Includes index.
1. Moving-picture actors and actresses—United
States—Biography. I. Title.
PN1998.A2M4 1982      791.43′028′0922      82-1217
ISBN: 0-517-376059                          AACR2

h g f e d

# TABLE OF CONTENTS

# DEDICATED
## With Affection And Respect To

**JACK NORTON**

**BESS FLOWERS**

. . . the Ultimate Drunk—And every other wonderful character player whose honored name and beloved face is absent from these pages because of the inexorable limitations of space.

. . . Veritable queen of the Dress Extras. And through her, to all those dear and familiar faces so fondly remembered . . . whose names we never knew.

# PREFACE

What a wonderful time it was — the era of the great rococo movie palaces of the past, before television had stripped movies of their position as the sole and supreme escape from the drabness of reality. Your ticket admitted you into a grotto-like world in which your anonymity was perfectly protected by the gentle enveloping darkness, though you were not alone by any means. From the moment you took your seat, you added your one unit of energy to the total electricity being generated by that mystical composite creature called an audience. And in return, its total energy flowed through you. In the same sense that the movie was larger than life, your reactions to it were also larger than life; for your laughter, your sympathy, or your tears merged with the same reaction of every other member of the audience, and came back to you, magnified a hundred-fold.

To insure that unanimity of response, every major studio had, in addition to its stars, a large stock company of character actors and bit players under contract. Like the stars, but to a lesser extent, their faces were their fortune. They were "types," and they turned up in movie after movie, playing virtually the same role over and over again. In time, their faces became almost as familiar to you as those of your own family, but unless you were a fanatic movie buff, you rarely knew their names. Just occasionally, some of them, like Walter Brennan, did indeed become stars; but for most of these players, the glamor and celebrity of stardom was forever beyond reach. Like the sidemen of an orchestra, or the linemen in football, they were the able professionals who carried out their assignments, making the stars look good, earning the respect of their fellow professionals, and only rarely sharing the glory of the limelight.

In a sense, they enacted the roles we moviegoers played in real life; and so, because they more nearly resembled us ordinary mortals, they were not as glamorous to us. The stars were like Gods — we could not really aspire to their enchanted lives, on or off the screen. So we lived out our fantasies through them, and rewarded them lavishly by permitting them the status of living legends. But as in real life, it was the supporting players who held those celluloid make-believe worlds together.

You see them on TV's late movies and you think to yourself: ". . . Who is that? . . . I've seen that face in a hundred movies . . . Who IS That?!"

Wonder no longer. For here are many of the most frequently seen players, categorized by their most frequently played role. If the identity of the assorted cops, cabbies, landladies, good-hearted tramps, stoolies, moppets, mad scientists and what have you is driving you mad as they flit across your TV screens; if you find yourself grinding your palm into your forehead and wondering, "WHO IS THAT?," then more likely than not, you'll get your answer here. For it is these wonderful characters who gave and continue to give so much pleasure who are the subject of this book. And within its covers anyway, they are Hollywood's brightest stars.

MY, Isn't She Cheap

IRIS ADRIAN

Your prissy maiden aunt very likely clucked her disapproval, but in her secret heart she probably loved these tough tomatoes too, for one could always see the heart of gold and the glint of good humor that lay just below the "hard," wise exterior. In their frizzy henna rinses, plucked and pencilled eyebrows, and too-generously applied lipstick, these ladies staffed countless dance halls, switchboards, and all-night diners. Generally too obvious or too comedic to play the "other woman," they usually starved for romance, although they were occasionally paired off with low, loveable brutes like Nat Pendleton, or seen as the moll of some featured hoodlum. In that latter context, they generally wound up dead, or at least bereaved. This was not a crowded category, and a walk among the counters of your nearest Woolworth's will probably reveal more specimens of the type than inhabited all of Hollywood.

GLADYS BLAKE

VEDA ANN BORG

JOYCE COMPTON

GLADYS GEORGE

MARIAN MARTIN

BEVERLY MICHAELS

ROBIN RAYMOND

OLGA SAN JUAN

| BILLIE BIRD | GRACE BRADLEY | CLAIRE CARLETON | INEZ COURTNEY | MYRNA DELL |
| GLORIA DICKSON | FIFI D'ORSAY | BEVERLY GARLAND | MAXINE GATES | MARY BETH HUGHES |
| ISABEL JEWELL | ARLINE JUDGE | PATSY KELLY | COLETTE LYONS | ADELE MARA |

MARIE McDONALD

MAYO METHOT

CLEO MOORE

DENNIE MOORE

ESTHER MUIR

ONA MUNSON

BARBARA NICHOLS

VIVIENNE OSBORNE

LEE PATRICK

BARBARA PEPPER

IRENE RYAN

ANN SAVAGE

MARTHA STEWART

MARIE WINDSOR

TOBY WING

KISS ME, YOU FOOL

HILLARY BROOKE

Many were the fools who succumbed to the leggy, athletic grace of Janis Carter, and her raincoat; the stunning coiffures and patrician nostrils of Andrea King; the glacial, hypnotic fascination of Gale Sondergaard. It took a true specialist to play that staple ingredient, the "Other Woman," for the actress had to edit out all that is endearing in the spectrum of woman — the suppliance, the yielding, the self-sacrifice, the softness — and focus in only on the hard and calculatedly self-seeking aspects of the feminine mystique. They provided romantic competition for the heroine, but they had no room for romance in their hearts for they were driven by vastly more greedy and selfish motivations. They didn't really want the man at all — he was just a necessary pre-requisite to satisfying their egos, their vanity, and their invariable lust for a lot of money. And because they were only fractions of total femininity, these lethal lovely ladies usually lost out. They may have been unloveable, but they certainly appeared to have captured the hearts of their makeup men, and in their lacquered perfection, they often resembled the sinister blossoms of some forbidden plant which enchants and then enslaves the weak and the unwary.

LYNN BARI

BINNIE BARNES

JANIS CARTER

KATHARINE DEMILLE

ROSE HOBART

PATRICIA MORISON

GAIL PATRICK

GALE SONDERGAARD

LOUISE ALLBRITTON

ASTRID ALLWYN

MARY ASTOR

STEPHANIE
BACHELOR

MONA BARRIE

HAZEL BROOKS

LESLIE BROOKS

PHYLLIS BROOKS

LILLIAN CORNELL

CLAIRE DODD

DORIS DOWLING

VIRGINIA FIELD

FRANCES GIFFORD

GLORIA HOLDEN

ADELE JERGENS

RITA JOHNSON

ANDREA KING

LOLA LANE

ANGELA LANSBURY

MONA MARIS

TRUDY MARSHALL

DOLORES MORAN

NATALIE MOREHEAD

BARBARA O'NEIL

GALE ROBBINS

LILYAN TASHMAN

CLAIRE TREVOR

JUNE VINCENT

HELEN VINSON

COBINA WRIGHT, JR.

These lovely and aristocratic ladies graced their simulated positions of wealth and power in dozens of films. Particularly during the Depression, it seemed to sooth and amuse the poor to watch the pecadillos of the idle rich, and Hollywood gladly obliged by manufacing a rash of comedies which allowed us to share vicariously the supposed lives of the privileged and well-born, as they worked and played.

Usually they played, for the movies appeared to be attempting to compensate the poor for their poverty by promulgating the notion that the rich were not too bright, or very useful. In addition, there was clearly the implication that a lot of money made you a bit whacky, for with the exception of the stuffier and older "dragons", like Lucile Watson, a high percentage of these ladies were singularly giddy and feather-headed. Certainly no one has every displayed more gullibility than Margaret Dumont, who regularly fell prey to the absurd strategems of Groucho Marx.

The rising tide of equality engulfed their crumbling way of life; their children invariably married "commoners"; and the species simply did not propogate itself. It's a very different world now, and these society woman exist only as anachronistic reminders of a more naive time, when the poor were a good deal more docile about it than they are today.

MARY BOLAND

CECIL CUNNINGHAM

MARJORIE GATESON

EDNA MAE OLIVER

MARJORIE RAMBEAU

NATALIE SCHAFER

NORMA VARDEN

LUCILE WATSON

MABEL ALBERTSON

KATHERINE
ALEXANDER

JANET BEECHER

ALICE BRADY

VIRGINIA BRISSAC

HELEN BRODERICK

LILLIAN BRONSON

BARBARA BROWN

NANA BRYANT

ILKA CHASE

LILLIAN CULVER

SARAH EDWARDS

MARY FORBES

KATHRYN GIVNEY

MINNA GOMBELL

| | | | | |
|---|---|---|---|---|
| LOUISE CLOSSER HALE | FRIEDA INESCORT | DORIS KENYON | ALMA KRUGER | JESSIE ROYCE LANDIS |
| DORIS LLOYD | CLAIRE MEADE | OTTOLA NESMITH | ISABEL RANDOLPH | ANN SHOEMAKER |
| ALLISON SKIPWORTH | VEREE TEASDALE | NELLA WALKER | JOSEPHINE WHITTELL | CORA WITHERSPOON |

Go Live From Children

ELIZABETH PATTERSON

18

Here we have a gallery of Mother's Day cards, warmly personified and brought to life on the screen by these beloved actresses, each of whom offered her own highly personalized interpretation of the maternal essence. And if your own mother is not represented here in prototype, then it is not because Hollywood failed to supply the widest possible choice of mother images for you to identify with.

That almost unlimited choice in styles of motherhood included: The stalwart stoicism of Anne Revere; the crusty sentimentality of Esther Dale; the careworn self-sacrifice of Dorothy Adams; the fey, imperishable girlishness of Spring Byington; the pragmatic common sense of Aline MacMahon; and the saintly grace of Fay Bainter. For those few of you whose mothers drank, it also included the alcoholic sweetness and tattered gallantry of Mabel Paige.

They gave Gibraltar-like support to their screen husbands, and they suffered the growing pains of their screen children, and forgave them as mothers the world over always do. And, as with your own mother, their sweetest rewards were probably best depicted in those magic moments when Mickey Rooney, as Andrew Hardy, looked into Fay Holden's eyes and fervently exclaimed: "Gee Mom — you're swell!"

FAY BAINTER

BEULAH BONDI

SPRING BYINGTON

JANE DARWELL

EMMA DUNN

FAY HOLDEN

IDA MOORE

MABEL PAIGE

DOROTHY ADAMS

MARJORIE BENNETT

MADGE BLAKE

CLARA BLANDICK

LAURA HOPE CREWS

ESTHER DALE

LOUISE DRESSER

BARBARA EVEREST

LUCILE GLEASON

SARA HADEN

KATHLEEN HOWARD

MARY KENT

KATHLEEN LOCKHART

ALINE MACMAHON

BERYL MERCER

20

MARY NASH

RUTH NELSON

SARA PADDEN

DOROTHY
PETERSON

MARY PHILLIPS

JESSIE RALPH

ANNE REVERE

ADELINE
DEWALT REYNOLDS

ELIZABETH RISDON

SELENA ROYLE

ZEFFIE TILBURY

DOROTHY VAUGHAN

NYDIA WESTMAN

MARGARET
WYCHERLY

MARY YOUNG

21

# Scram Kid, You Bother Me

MARCIA MAE JONES

Adorable, bewitching, appealing — those were some of the adjectives used to describe these precocious moppets. If you were a child yourself at the time, you probably didn't feel much kinship with them. With a child's directness, you perceived that they weren't really the genuine article, but were like coins which Hollywood had minted in commemoration of childhood.

Some of these kids were truly remarkable and could almost break the barrier which separates memorizing from acting. A few, like Roddy McDowell, Elizabeth Taylor, and Natalie Wood, have gone on to achieve an impressive adult artistry. Others have vanished into adult anonymity. But for all of them, there is a celluloid Shangri-La in which they are forever young — a Charlie McCarthy with their features, who exists in the past, and never grows old.

Just for fun, try turning the sound all the way down the next time you watch a Shirley Temple movie. You will see a sensuality as broad and as full-blown as that of Marilyn Monroe, or even Mae West. Perhaps it was some of these diminutive co-workers that W. C. Fields had in mind when he remarked that anyone who hated animals and children couldn't be all bad.

One thing is certain though — your own childhood was probably happier than theirs.

PEGGY ANN GARNER

SYBIL JASON

GIGI PERREAU

VIRGINIA WEIDLER

SCOTTY BECKETT

BUTCH JENKINS

TERRY KILBURN

DEAN STOCKWELL

JOAN CARROLL

ANN CARTER

CORA SUE COLLINS

CAROLYN LEE

CONNIE MARSHALL

SHARON MCMANUS

LAURIE LEE MICHEL

SHARYN MOFFETT

PATSY NASH

JANINE PERREAU

PAT PREST

BABY SANDY

BEVERLY
SUE SIMMONS

ANN TODD

JANIS WILSON

TED DONALDSON

BOBBY DRISCOLL

FARINA

DARRYL HICKMAN

JIMMY HUNT

TOMMY KELLY

SPANKY
MACFARLAND

DICKIE MOORE

LARRY NUNN

BILLY SEVERN

JOHNNY SHEFFIELD

LARRY SIMMS

CARL
"ALFALFA" SWITZER

BOBS WATSON

GEORGE
'FOGHORN' WINSLOW

GLORIA DEHAVEN

JEFF DONNELL

ANN GILLIS

BONITA GRANVILLE

BRENDA HENDERSON

GLORIA JEAN

BARBARA ANN JONES

BETTY LYNN

JEAN PORTER

JUNE PREISSER

JUANITA QUIGLEY

JOYCE REYNOLDS

BARBARA RUICK

ANN RUTHERFORD

PEGGY RYAN

HERBERT ANDERSON

KENNY BOWERS

STANLEY CLEMENTS

LEO GORCEY

HUNTZ HALL

BILLY HALOP

SKIP HOMEIER

RICHARD JAEKEL

CONRAD JANIS

JIMMY LYDON

RAY MCDONALD

CHARLES SMITH

RUSS TAMBLYN

LOREN TINDALL

LEON TYLER

The intrusive ladies and gentlemen of this category elevated the art of minding everybody else's business to undreamed-of heights of perfection.

The female of the species were virtuoso snoops and gossips — far deadlier than the male. Admittedly there were some like Marie Blake and Mary Treen, who were well-intentioned enough — and while they didn't help, they really meant no harm. But the overwhelming majority, like Margaret Hamilton and Hope Emerson, had long sharp noses, trained to point to whatever trouble you might be in. And even more to their liking was the trouble they could cause with their caustic and malevolent tongues, from their vantage points as Landladies, Spinsters and the Shrewish Wives of henpecked husbands.

The men tended rather uniformly to be nervous, prissy little fussbudgets, operating with maddening officiousness within the small authority of a minor clerkdom. They infested the front desks of a legion of hotels; relentlessly served summonses on the people you liked; and closed marriage bureaus promptly at five. Their mission in life was to uphold the letter of the law, not its spirit.

But the saving grace of all these busybodies lay in the certainty that somewhere along the line, they would be satisfyingly foiled, leaving the plot unencumbered and on its way to a happy ending.

FLORENCE BATES

CONNIE GILCHRIST

MARGARET HAMILTON

ALMIRA SESSIONS

RICHARD HAYDN

EDWARD EVERETT HORTON

DONALD MEEK

GRADY SUTTON

| | | | | |
|---|---|---|---|---|
| MARIE BLAKE | ELLEN CORBY | RUTH DONNELLY | HOPE EMERSON | FERN EMMETT |
| KATHLEEN FREEMAN | VICTORIA HORNE | ROSALIND IVAN | ANNE O'NEAL | RENIE RIANO |
| VIRGINIA SALE | MARY TREEN | MINERVA URECAL | VERA VAGUE | MARY WICKES |

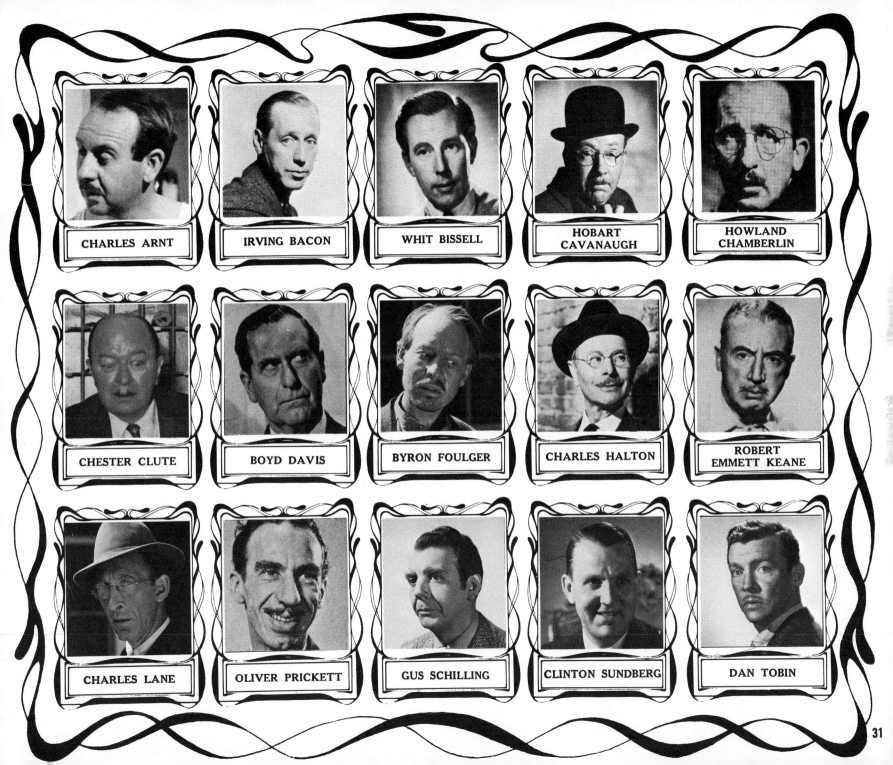

CHARLES ARNT

IRVING BACON

WHIT BISSELL

HOBART
CAVANAUGH

HOWLAND
CHAMBERLIN

CHESTER CLUTE

BOYD DAVIS

BYRON FOULGER

CHARLES HALTON

ROBERT
EMMETT KEANE

CHARLES LANE

OLIVER PRICKETT

GUS SCHILLING

CLINTON SUNDBERG

DAN TOBIN

31

DON'T TRUST THIS MAN

DOUGLASS DUMBRILLE

32

Instant automatic distrust was the quality purveyed by each of these gentlemen. They came in all shapes and sizes and on every level of the social structure. There were Upper-Crust Insufferables like Henry Daniell; Well-Oiled Smoothies with an aura of decadent seedy grandeur about them like George Zucco and Douglass Dumbrille; Babbitt Business Types like Charles Dingle; Mean-Tempered Working Stiffs like Victor Killian; High-School Dropouts with leadership qualities like Ted deCorsia and Douglas Fowley; and Welfare Unlovelies like Abner Biberman and Walter Burke. And then there were society's scum, a breed of specialists, each of whom possessed a personal, trade-marked repulsiveness. These included vermin like Berry Kroeger; slime like Alan Baxter; yechhh! like Dan Seymour; sadistic plug-uglies like Jack Lambert; and monstrous grotesques like Rondo Hatton. But whenever and however you saw them, even when they were trying to be nice, your hackles bristled, your suspicions were aroused, and the warning signals immediately went up in your subconscious. They read: DON'T TRUST THIS MAN.

**EDUARDO CIANNELLI**

**GEORGE COULOURIS**

**HENRY DANIELL**

**VICTOR FRANCEN**

**BERRY KROEGER**

**SHELDON LEONARD**

**GEORGE MACREADY**

**GEORGE ZUCCO**

LIONEL ATWILL

ALAN BAXTER

ABNER BIBERMAN

WALTER BURKE

JOHN CARRADINE

PAUL CAVANAUGH

HOWARD DA SILVA

TED DE CORSIA

CHARLES DINGLE

JACK ELAM

DOUGLAS FOWLEY

RONDO HATTON

JOHN HOYT

HAROLD HUBER

VICTOR JORY

CY KENDALL

VICTOR KILLIAN

JACK LAMBERT

JACK LARUE

MARC LAWRENCE

IAN MACDONALD

BARTON MACLANE

MIKE MAZURKI

ROBERT MIDDLETON

GAVIN MUIR

DAN SEYMOUR

LEE VAN CLEEF

PHILIP VAN ZANDT

GRANT WITHERS

IAN WOLFE

He Should Have Stood in Bed

ELISHA COOK, JR.

In the movies, as in life, there are many losers for every winner. This category was so plentifully supplied that we cannot even begin to concern ourselves with those who merely lost the girl. The gentlemen you see here made their comfortable livelihoods by regularly losing life, limb, family, reputation, and property.

They lost to the Indians, the Russians, the Nazis, the Japanese, Mother Nature, and sometimes, even to each other. They got shot, stabbed, tortured, evicted, maimed by their own farm implements; and if no one else bothered to do them in, they often obligingly committed suicide.

Some deserved to lose, and some did not. It was pleasurable to watch the repellant Elisha Cook Jr. get his; whereas the tragic plight of a hapless John Qualen usually evoked your pity. At the comic end of the scale, there were the loveable professional "stupids" like Rags Ragland, Nat Pendleton, and Warren Hymer, who always got amusingly outwitted — or perhaps more aptly, out half-witted.

But whatever the circumstances, losing was the name of the game, and the predictable fate of each of these gentlemen. Defeat was a trademark stamped indelibly on their features, and from the moment they came on the screen, you just knew they had little or no future.

WALTER BALDWIN

WOLFE BARZELL

J. EDWARD BROMBERG

PAUL GUILFOYLE

PERCY HELTON

NAT PENDLETON

JOHN QUALEN

LUIS VAN ROOTEN

JOHN ABBOTT

TREVOR BARDETTE

VINCE BARNETT

DON BEDDOE

PAUL E. BURNS

FRANK CADY

ANTHONY CARUSO

GEORGE CHANDLER

ALEC CRAIG

ROBERT DUDLEY

WILLIAM EDMUNDS

THOMAS FADDEN

FRANK FERGUSON

PAUL FIX

JAMES GRIFFITH

| PORTER HALL | DAVID HOFFMAN | ARTHUR HUNNICUTT | WARREN HYMER | GENE LOCKHART |

| JON LORMER | LOU LUBIN | ED MAX | JAMES MILLICAN | FRANCIS PIERLOT |

| RAGS RAGLAND | RUSSELL SIMPSON | HAROLD VERMILYEA | EDDIE WALLER | O. Z. WHITEHEAD |

THURSTON HALL

Everyone of these windy gentlemen had a genial streak of larceny in his soul. And even when they were lobbying in behalf of perfectly legitimate and decent causes, it still sounded like some sort of sneaky con. They "put-on" everybody, but the choicest moments came when they put each other on in epic duels of chicanery. Each master stylist had his favorite weapon, and their aggregate arsenal included the Bluster of Thurston Hall; the Bucolic Shrewdness (and sheer age) of Clem Bevans; the Insidious Smugness of Howard Freeman; the Sleazy Cunning of Walter Catlett; and the Transparent Hokum of Raymond Walburn.

They made difficult husbands, and their children tended to view them either with shame, rebellion, or tolerant amusement. And when conniving failed and bluster was unavailing, these old rascals could afford to accept defeat gracefully, for they knew they'd be back to delight us once again with a verbal barrage of hrumphs, and another obvious hustle.

CLEM BEVANS

WALTER CATLETT

LEON ERROL

GUY KIBBEE

CLARENCE KOLB

EUGENE PALLETTE

ANDREW TOMBES

RAYMOND WALBURN

JOHN ALEXANDER     EDWARD ARNOLD     GEORGE BARBIER     EDGAR BUCHANAN     FRED CLARK

GEORGE CLEVELAND     LLOYD CORRIGAN     WILLIAM DEMAREST     RALPH DUMKE     DICK ELLIOT

FRANK FAYLEN     WALLACE FORD     WILLIAM FRAWLEY     HOWARD FREEMAN     BILLY GILBERT

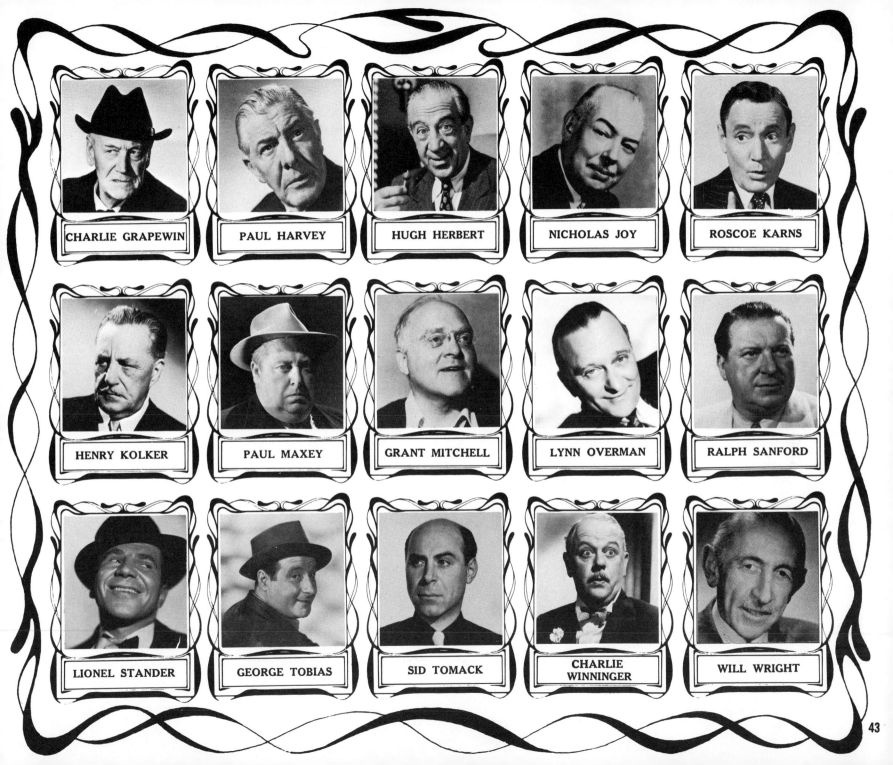

CHARLIE GRAPEWIN

PAUL HARVEY

HUGH HERBERT

NICHOLAS JOY

ROSCOE KARNS

HENRY KOLKER

PAUL MAXEY

GRANT MITCHELL

LYNN OVERMAN

RALPH SANFORD

LIONEL STANDER

GEORGE TOBIAS

SID TOMACK

CHARLIE WINNINGER

WILL WRIGHT

43

Everybody's Good Ol' Gramps

HARRY DAVENPORT

Gazing into the collective faces of these upstanding senior citizens, one is almost overwhelmed by the sheer mass of benign integrity that gazes back. True, Ray Collins might occasionally sell guns to the Indians; Moroni Olsen might carry scientific research into sinister areas; and Ernest Truex might impishly pinch his nurse; but by and large, Hollywood scrupulously honored the principle of respect for one's elders, and a silver thatch usually adorned a wise old head.

These distinguished gentlemen were usually more convincing as bankers, judges, military commanders and board chairmen, than their real-life counterparts — certainly they were almost always better looking, in that limited style of photogenic male maturity that has become a cliché of retirement insurance advertising. Further-more, their good looks did not particularly appear to be the product of graceful aging, for in some eerie way, they appeared never to have been young; and in compensation, they seemed never to age within their seniority.

Now and again they might allude fondly to some cherished memory of youthful hell-raising, but you had to take their word for it, for there remained not a vestige of anything but rock-ribbed, almost biblical decency.

They were truly "Everybody's Good Ol' Gramps," and if they seem highly euphemistic versions of your own Grandfather, it is probably because the movies were less concerned with life as it is, than they were with life as it ought to be.

RUSSELL HICKS    SAMUEL S. HINES    HENRY O'NEIL    ADDISON RICHARDS

C. AUBREY SMITH    HENRY STEPHENSON    LEWIS STONE    HENRY TRAVERS

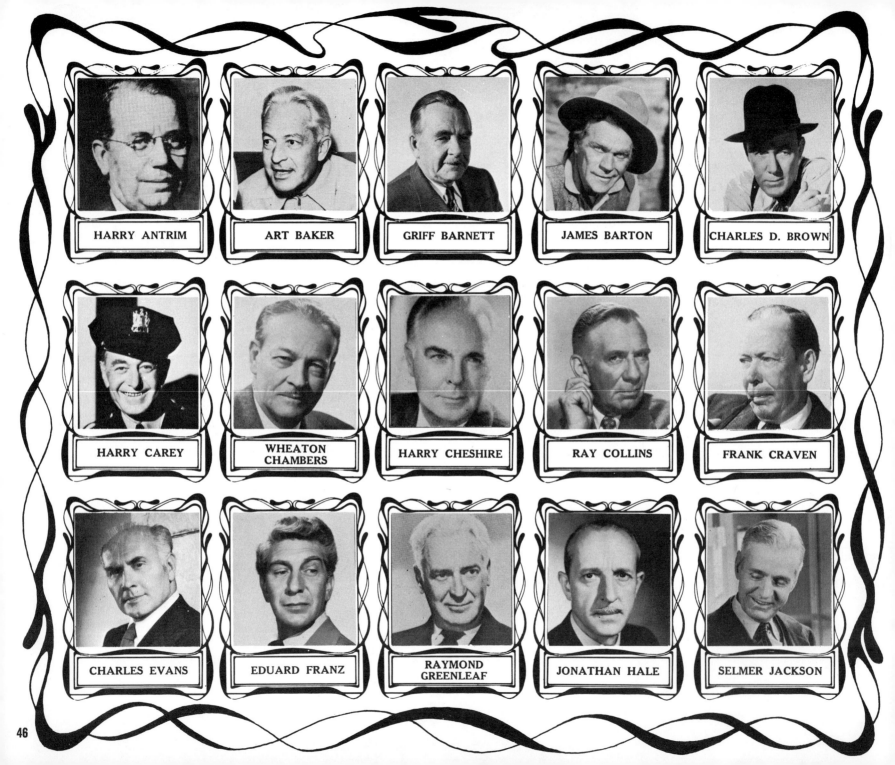

HARRY ANTRIM

ART BAKER

GRIFF BARNETT

JAMES BARTON

CHARLES D. BROWN

HARRY CAREY

WHEATON CHAMBERS

HARRY CHESHIRE

RAY COLLINS

FRANK CRAVEN

CHARLES EVANS

EDUARD FRANZ

RAYMOND GREENLEAF

JONATHAN HALE

SELMER JACKSON

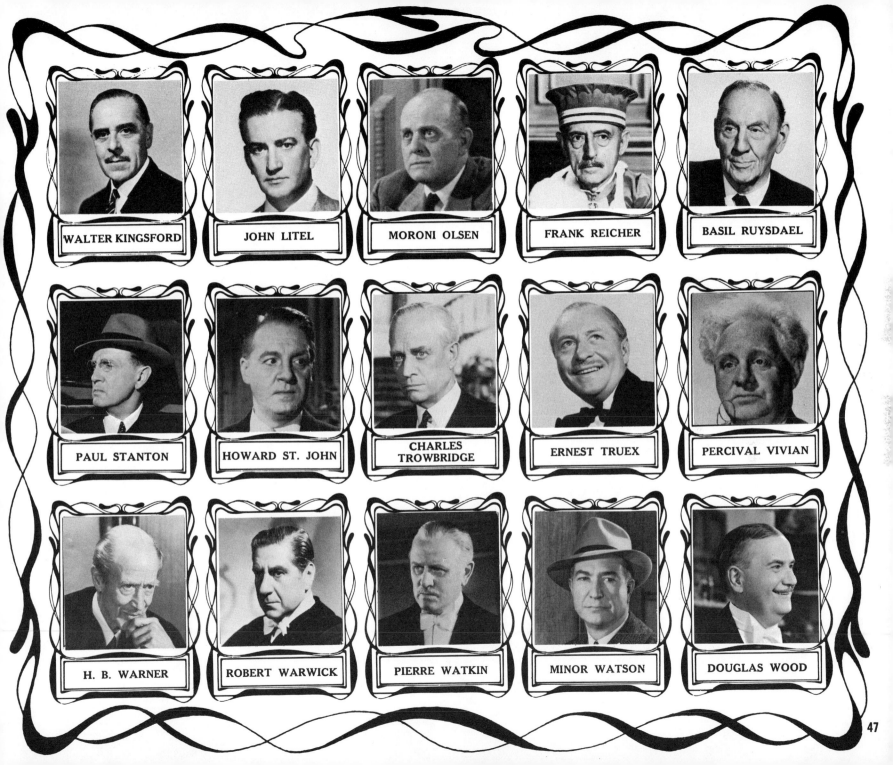

WALTER KINGSFORD

JOHN LITEL

MORONI OLSEN

FRANK REICHER

BASIL RUYSDAEL

PAUL STANTON

HOWARD ST. JOHN

CHARLES
TROWBRIDGE

ERNEST TRUEX

PERCIVAL VIVIAN

H. B. WARNER

ROBERT WARWICK

PIERRE WATKIN

MINOR WATSON

DOUGLAS WOOD

Ethnic types were the backbone of War movies, Spy yarns, Historical films, and Situation comedies. Each face was unmistakably a map of its country of origin, (whether it had originated there or not). One could instantly accept Mischa Auer as a phony Russian Prince; Conrad Veidt as a Nazi General; Donald Macbride as an Irish Cop; or J. Carroll Naish as an Italian anything. The British Colony graced us with lovely ladies like Gladys Cooper; impeccable gentlemen like Reginald Denny; and even more impeccable gentlemen's gentlemen like Halliwell Hobbes.

In an era with a vastly different social consciousness, it was possible to enjoy Willie Best without guilt, and to hate Richard Loo without pity.

Space does not permit more than a smattering of the Miscellaneous Ethnics who peopled our films, and so Chief Yowlachie must stand as the solitary representative of all the Indians who fell as the railways moved west. Along with him, you will also find Sabu, Marvin Kaplan, and the ubiquitous Louis Jean Heydt, who turned up as everything but a woman.

JAMES GLEASON

NIGEL BRUCE

J. CARROLL NAISH

WILLIE BEST

CONRAD VEIDT

AKIM TAMIROFF

RICHARD LOO

TURHAN BEY

SARA ALLGOOD

MARY BOYD

MARY GORDON

HOPE LANDIN

UNA O'CONNOR

EDWARD S. BROPHY

JAMES BURKE

JIMMY CONLIN

EDGAR DEARING

TOM DUGAN

JAMES FLAVIN

EDWARD GARGAN

ALAN HALE

ROBERT HOMANS

PAUL HURST

ALLEN JENKINS | FRANK JENKS | EDGAR KENNEDY | TOM KENNEDY | J. M. KERRIGAN

DONALD MACBRIDE | FRANK MCHUGH | MATT MCHUGH | FRANK ORTH | TIM RYAN

JOE SAWYER | HARRY SHANNON | ARTHUR SHIELDS | FRANK SULLY | RHYS WILLIAMS

CONSTANCE COLLIER

GLADYS COOPER

ISOBEL ELSOM

ETHEL GRIFFIES

MARTITA HUNT

ELSA LANCHESTER

EILY MALYON

CATHLEEN NESBITT

FLORA ROBSON

DAME MAY WHITTY

ERIC BLORE

LEO G. CARROLL

MELVILLE COOPER

ERNEST COSSART

DONALD CRISP

ROLAND CULVER

REGINALD DENNY

REGINALD GARDNER

SIR CEDRIC HARDWICKE

DENNIS HOEY

HALLIWELL HOBBES

CECIL KELLAWAY

MILES MANDER

AUBREY MATHER

ROBERT MORLEY

ALAN MOWBRAY

ALAN NAPIER

REGINALD OWEN

ARTHUR TREACHER

ROLAND YOUNG

ARGENTINA
BRUNETTI

IPHOGENIE
CASTIGLIONI

AUGUSTA CIOLLI

ANN CODEE

ESTHER MINCIOTTI

LUIS ALBERNI

ALPHONSO BEDOYA

FORTUNIO
BONANOVA

JOSEPH CALLEIA

LEO CARRILLO

MAURICE CASS

JEAN DE BRIAC

PEDRO
DE CORDOBA

JOE DOMINGUEZ

ANTONIO FILAURI

54

| | | | | |
|---|---|---|---|---|
| NACHO GALINDO | MARTIN GARRALAGA | JOSE ITURBI | CHARLES LA TORRE | CHRIS PIN MARTIN |
| LOUIS MERCIER | ALEX MONTOYA | NESTOR PAIVA | NINO PIPITONE | FRANK PUGLIA |
| PEDRO REGAS | JULIAN RIVERO | MARIO SILETTI | JOSE TORVAY | FRANK YACONELLI |

LOUISE BEAVERS

MARIETTA CANTY

WILLA
PEARL CURTIS

RUBY DANDRIDGE

RUBY GOODWIN

JESSIE GRAYSON

THERESA HARRIS

ETTA MCDANIEL

HATTIE MCDANIEL

NINA MAE
MCKINNEY

BUTTERFLY
MCQUEEN

JUANITA MOORE

MADIE NORMAN

LILLIAN RANDOLPH

LIBBY TAYLOR

ROBERT DAVIS

STEPIN FETCHIT

JUANO HERNANDEZ

J. LOUIS JOHNSON

SAM (DEACON) McDANIEL

MANTAN MORELAND

CLARENCE MUSE

NICODEMUS

FREDERICK O'NEAL

GEORGE REED

CLINTON ROSEMOND

BILL WALKER

LEIGH WHIPPER

DOOLEY WILSON

ERNEST WILSON

SIG ARNO

ALBERT BASSERMAN

FELIX BRESSART

LUDWIG DONATH

FRITZ FELD

HUGO HAAS

KURT KATCH

MARTIN KOSLECK

KURT KREUGER

TORBEN MEYER

OTTO PREMINGER

SIG RUMAN

LUDWIG STOSSEL

IVAN TRIESAULT

ERIC
VON STROHEIM

OLGA
BACLANOVA

FERIKE BOROS

KASIA
ORZAZEWSKI

MARIA
OUSPENSKAYA

GISELA
WERBISECK

MISCHA AUER

LEON BELASCO

STEVEN GERAY

OSCAR HOMOLKA

LEONID KINSKY

CHARLES KORVIN

MIKHAIL RASUMNY

GREGORY RATOFF

S. Z. SAKALL

VLADIMIR
SOKOLOFF

PHILIP AHN

PETER CHONG

BENSON FONG

HAROLD FONG

WING FOO

WILLIE FUNG

JAMES HONG

ROBERT KINO

EDDIE LEE

KEYE LUKE

TERU SHIMADA

LEONARD STRONG

KAM TONG

H. T. TSIANG

SEN YUNG

OSA MASSEN

ANNA Q. NILSSON

VERA
HRUBA RALSTON

HELENE THIMIG

JEAN WONG

NILS ASTHER

PHILIP DORN

CARL ESMOND

LOUIS
JEAN HEYDT

MARVIN KAPLAN

GEORGE KHOURY

FRITZ LEIBER

HARRY ROSENTHAL

SABU

CHIEF YOWLACHIE

# ALPHABETICAL INDEX

# ABOUT THE AUTHOR

WARREN B. MEYERS

There is no truth to the rumor that Warren B. Meyers is actually three people, although this talented and remarkably versatile native New Yorker has indeed functioned at or near the top of a dazzling variety of careers.

As a musician, he was for several years one of the country's leading arranger-conductors, and among its more sought-after creators of night club acts and special material. In this capacity, he lent his considerable talents to Diahann Carroll, Marlene Dietrich, Connie Francis, Jose Ferrer, The Hallmark Hall of Fame, and a glittering galaxy of others. His excellence as a jazz pianist has earned him the rare distinction of having appeared with the Count Basie Orchestra in New York's famed Carnegie Hall.

As an actor, his credits include the Broadway productions of *Me and Juliet, Compulsion,* and *Lenny;* plus a national tour of *The Owl and the Pussycat,* in which he co-starred, to rave reviews, opposite Pat Suzuki. His is one of the busier voices of radio and television commercials, and he frequently turns up on such daytime soap operas as *Love of Life, All My Children, Somerset,* and *Edge of Night.*

As a writer and/or composer, he has supplied material for many television shows, several commercial products, and a battery of off-Broadway revues. Broadway musicals are his ultimate goal, and while all of his efforts to date in this area have been optioned for production, none of them has yet made it successfully to that hallowed ground. However, he intends, in his own words, to "hang in there until either success or death occur—preferably in that order."

As president of Production Design Associates, Inc., he heads a firm as versatile as he is, which dreams up, packages, and produces virtually anything that strikes them as a good idea.

He is, in short, a jack of many trades who has managed to master most of them.